A STONE'S THROW

Living with a Loved One's Depression

Kay J. Cee

Published by
Innovo Publishing, LLC
www.innovopublishing.com
1-888-546-2111

innovo
PUBLISHING

Providing Full-Service Publishing Services for
Christian Authors, Artists & Organizations: Hardbacks, Paperbacks,
eBooks, Audiobooks, Music & Film

A STONE'S THROW
Living with a Loved One's Depression
Copyright © 2013 by Kay J. Cee
All rights reserved.

Scripture quotations are taken from the *Holy Bible,* New Living Translation,
Copyright © 1996, 2004, 2007 by Tyndale House Foundation. Used by
permission of Tyndale House Publishers, Inc., Carol Stream,
Illinois 60188. All rights reserved.

ISBN 13: 978-1-61314-128-1

Cover Design & Interior Layout: Innovo Publishing, LLC

Printed in the United States of America
U.S. Printing History

First Edition: February 2013

PREFACE

I want you to know that I did not take the responsibility of writing this book lightly. It is such a personal story that I often hesitated to put it into words. But I have always held a strong belief that God has a reason that I am still here on this earth. I have a purpose to fulfill, something He set aside just for me.

My family and friends have encouraged me to write my story. They, and I, believe that it is a story that may help someone. I have always thought that if I could stand in front of God one day and He could look at me and say, "Well done," then my life would have been worth living.

I did not use my real name in this book. While it is my story to tell and I am hoping it will help people, I do not live my life alone. My life has touched so many other lives that I do not feel it right to share their story; that is their decision to make. For their privacy, I have not shared the details of their lives. While my husband wishes he did not have to be the catalyst for this book, I told him that it may be our purpose to bring attention to this illness, to bring light to a subject that often stays hidden in the darkness.

TABLE OF CONTENTS

Why—The Beginning 9

The Stone's Throw—His Side, His Feelings 17

Circles—My Side, My Feelings 25

Ever-Widening Circles—The Other Side 45

Circles Within Circles—A Mother's Worry 67

Still Waters 73

Inspirations 81

Acknowledgments 85

Additional Resources 87

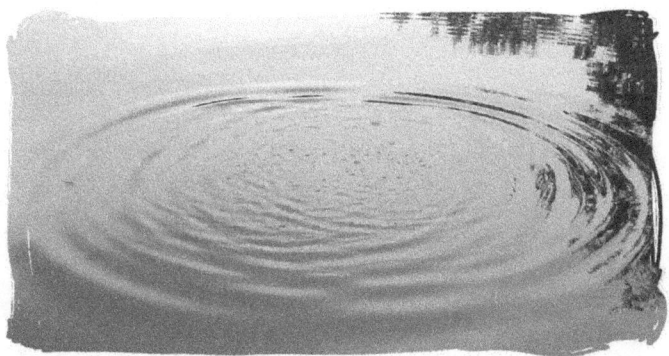

Depression is like a pebble thrown in a lake.
The pebble sinks, while the water swirls
around it, circling, ever circling, unable
to break away and escape its force. It is
drawn in by its power, helpless to
stop being drawn down with it.

*"The deep waters gushed over them; they sank to the
bottom like a stone."*
(Exodus 15:5)

WHY

The Beginning

My husband and I were living our lives, raising our kids, and doing our jobs. Then something brought a complete shift to our lives—an illness that brought our fairly even life to a stop. We have since been forced to look at our lives and make some tough decisions. There have been struggles, tears, fears, blame, guilt, and breakdowns. This book is for the often forgotten and overlooked caregivers, the ones in the midst of it all trying to keep balance in the middle of chaos.

I have struggled for years to put into words how it felt to be in the middle of this and have wrestled whether I should open up to others who might be going through it also. It is very personal, and I have always been a very private person. However, I feel that God is allowing these things to happen for a reason. If one person reads this and feels a little less alone, then this was worth it. God has seen me through a lot of trials in my life, and I have always had faith that they were all for His glory. This story, as painful as it is to tell, will show that God still has not forsaken me, and has led me to a new appreciation of every day He gives me.

This hateful illness seemed to come out of nowhere, swooping down and disrupting our lives. Most people are unable to pinpoint that defining moment when their lives began to change; we certainly couldn't. It can creep up slowly, noticing small changes day by day. It can happen in the space of a couple of hours. Over the years, it has seemed to happen both ways.

If you have ever loved anyone going through a life-changing illness, you know the feelings of helplessness, anger, and despair. I don't mean just their feelings; I am talking about your own. We feel all this and more, yet we also have such guilt. Who are we to have these feelings? We are not the ones suffering through the illness. We are not the patient. Where do we find help when we are not the sick one? Are you selfish for having these feelings, for feeling so confused, so lost? Where do you get off wanting comfort when they are the ones in pain?

You search for validation for feeling the way you do, for someone to tell you it's okay to feel like this. A lot of people will tell you that you have to stay strong. You have to stand beside your loved one because they need you. Most people will not recognize the pain, fear, and loneliness that you are dealing with. They only see your role in helping the person who is sick. They do not, cannot, or will not acknowledge your pain and frustration.

When my life felt like it was being torn apart day by day, I went everywhere searching for information to help me. I needed something to let me know that there was another person out there who felt these same feelings and asked these same questions. I was too embarrassed to ask anyone else. I was afraid of how they might judge him, me, or us. I didn't know how to bring the subject up. Do I just open up the conversation with, "Hey, my husband has been suffering from depression, and I think I am going crazy trying to deal with it. Have you got any suggestions?" You probably won't get the answers you were hoping for!

I was afraid of people's reactions. But in the process of writing this book, God has placed many wonderful people in my path who have encouraged me and given me the courage to complete this part of my journey. I found that many people struggle through an illness alone, afraid to open up to others. That neighbor or co-worker sitting next to you may be struggling silently, unaware that someone so near is struggling also. Why do we work so hard to hide our struggles? Why are we so afraid of others judging us?

"So let's stop condemning each other. Decide instead to live in such a way that you will not cause another believer to stumble and fall" (Romans 14:13).

Just remember; you can't control what other people will think or act.

"So why do you condemn another believer? Why do you look down on another believer? Remember, we will all stand before the judgment seat of God" (Romans 14:10).

I did find books and articles for people going through depression, but I couldn't find any book to help the people who loved and cared for them. Where were the books to help us, a book to answer our questions? What about how we feel? Will we ever get our lives back? What is normal? Will we ever laugh again?

Where is the help for the ones who are suffering along with their loved ones, the ones who are down in the abyss with them? Where is the book to tell us that our feelings of abandonment, panic, helplessness, guilt, and yes, even anger, are normal reactions? That these feelings we have are not evil, uncaring, or selfish. That we are entitled to have them, and they are legitimate feelings. I needed something or someone to tell me that I had the right to feel this way and others had felt this way too. The main thing I needed to know was that I was not alone.

I am not a doctor or counselor. I don't have the solutions to depression. All I have is the reassurance that others share some of the feelings you may be experiencing and that you are not alone. You might be desperate for someone to talk to about your feelings but maybe fear, privacy, lack of understanding, and even shame has left you with no one to talk to.

Writing this book came from that desperate search for help and advice. I pray that this will help someone else realize that they are not alone in their feelings and that others have experienced them also. I also pray that you will learn from my mistakes, as I have tried to do.

When I began this book, I was concerned about opening up what was, and is, a very personal time in our lives. I found these verses in my Bible that sums up my reason for writing about what we are going through and confirmed to me that it was the right thing to do.

"All praise to God, the Father of our LORD Jesus Christ. God is our merciful Father and the source of all comfort. He comforts us in all our troubles so that we can comfort others. When they are troubled, we will be able to give them the same comfort God has given us" (2 Corinthians 1:3–4).

"God blesses those who patiently endure testing and temptation. Afterward they will receive the crown of life that God has promised to those who love him" (James 1:12).

I pray that one day you too can follow this and pass it on to another one who needs comfort.

This is my story of living with depression, his and eventually mine too. What started out as a search to find a reason for that illness actually ended with the discovery of *me*.

A stone entering the water with such force as to create ever-widening circles, imprisoning all it encounters.

"You have thrown me into the lowest pit, into the darkest depths." (Psalm 88:6)

THE STONE'S THROW

His Side, His Feelings

•————————————————————————————•

Over the years, I have asked him numerous times to try to explain it to me. To explain how he feels when he is going through this. To tell me how it starts and when he knows it is back. But he has always said he is too tired or too busy, any excuse to avoid discussing it. He did not want to talk about it.

Now, many years later, we have looked back and tried to recall those feelings that, at the time, seemed impossible for him to express, at least not in terms that we on the outside could understand.

This is the inside story, short as it may be, of how the person you love may be feeling, the feelings of anguish and despair that they are experiencing but may be unable to put into words.

He says it starts with an anxious feeling, similar to butterflies in the pit of your stomach that won't go away. He wakes up with that feeling and has to continually fight the urge to roll back over and go back to sleep. During sleep, he doesn't have to deal with anything. If he does make it to his job, he will hurry through the day. He hurries to get back home to his safe haven. Back home he can try to relax and to calm the anxiousness. Most days, he makes it home only to go straight back to bed. Some days, he will have to leave work early because he has a terrible headache. Other days, he can't make it to work at all. During an episode of depression, bed seems to be the only place where he feels comfortable. He will sleep **a lot.** I think that is one of the first signs you may notice—his or her desire to be alone.

The odd thing about the constant sleeping is that he tells me he is always tired! He's tired when he comes home, so he goes straight to bed. Twelve hours later, he wakes up and says he's exhausted. It is a never-ending cycle.

It is like living in a constant rainy, overcast day, those days that never see sunshine. Everywhere I look, I see shades of gray. If a ray of sun manages to slip through, it is quickly eclipsed by another cloud.

When searching through my Bible, I found Psalm 38. It seems to capture what I imagine depression to feel like. I do not think depression is the result of sin; I simply chose this because of the deep emotions expressed in its verses. They describe the anguish and despair that engulfs you and the weight you carry on your shoulders, how you are always searching for rest or somewhere to lay down this burden.

O Lord, don't rebuke me in your anger or discipline me in your rage! Your arrows have struck deep, and your blows are crushing me. Because of your anger, my whole body is sick; my health is broken because of my sins. My guilt overwhelms me—it is a burden too heavy to bear.

My wounds fester and stink because of my foolish sins. I am bent over and racked with pain. All day long I walk around filled with grief. A raging fever burns within me, and my health is broken. I am exhausted and completely crushed. My groans come from an anguished heart.

You know what I long for, Lord; you hear my every sigh. My heart beats wildly, my strength fails, and I am going blind. My loved ones and friends stay away, fearing my disease. Even my own family stands at a distance. Meanwhile, my enemies lay traps to kill me. Those who wish me harm make plans to ruin me. All day long they plan their treachery.

But I am deaf to all their threats. I am silent before them as one who cannot speak. I choose to hear nothing, and I make no reply. For I am waiting for you, O Lord. You must answer for me, O Lord my God. I prayed, "Don't let my enemies gloat over me or rejoice at my downfall."

I am on the verge of collapse, facing constant pain. But I confess my sins; I am deeply sorry for what I have done. I have many aggressive enemies; they hate me without reason. They repay me evil for good and oppose me for pursuing good.
Do not abandon me, O Lord. Do not stand at a distance, my God. Come quickly to help me, O Lord my savior (Psalm 38).

He has an endless list of "aches." The most common one is a headache. He had an MRI and thankfully, nothing showed up. He had a complete workup, six vials of blood tested for various things, and still nothing. But what I noticed each time a test result came back was that he appeared disappointed they didn't find anything. Most people are thrilled when they get those results, but not a person suffering from depression. They seem to crave some sort of test result that will point out a specific ailment that can be treated, something concrete that they can point to and say, "That's it; that's why I feel like do."

And as much as it hurts, some days I find myself wanting the same thing.

He tells me over and over again what I prize I got when I married him. He apologizes constantly about being this way. Sometimes I think he means it sarcastically, and other times I think he just wants, more than anything, for me to tell him it isn't true.

"Now, however, it is time to forgive and comfort him. Otherwise he may be overcome by discouragement. So I urge you now to reaffirm your love for him" (2 Corinthians 2:7–8).

He has finally admitted that after all these years, he was only aware of one side of things. He felt like he went through every hardship in his life completely alone. He said he was never aware of all the times I was there beside him. He believed that he faced every trial by himself. That took me completely by surprise! For all those times where I tried to be strong for him to lean on, he never even realized I was there. It took him years to finally see that I was by his side all along.

No one knows what they are going to face when they become a couple. No one can foresee the trials, frustrations, anger, and hurt that might lie ahead. No one can see the joy, smiles, laughs, and shared memories that lie ahead either. You go into a relationship not knowing the future. Your wedding vows say for richer, for poorer, in sickness and in health, but you never think about those words until something happens to make you realize that you did make a vow, to your spouse and to God. But isn't that what life is all about? You take that step out into the unknown. You step out and trust God to know the path and to lead you where He wants you to go. No, I never would have imagined that this is where our path would lead us. But here we are.

Maybe God put us on this path to open our eyes to others who are suffering. I see that same look in others' eyes that I have seen in his. I recognize that dark look. The monotone voice that speaks way more than what they are actually saying. I now try to say something to encourage without pressuring. I try to express my caring without overstepping. I pray for the right words to say, for the right tone in my voice, and the right look in my eyes. I just pray. If this is what God wants me to do, I pray that I am doing it right in His eyes.

Is this ever going to go away?

I don't think it will ever completely leave our lives. It is forever like a shadow lurking in the corners, waiting for the time to reappear. We just continue every day, thankful for the good days.

Trusting . . .

What is going on? I want my life back!
I want our life back!

*"Don't let the floods overwhelm me, or the deep waters
swallow me, or the pit of death devour me."
(Psalm 69:15)*

CIRCLES

My Side, My Feelings

⟢──⟣

I felt like my life was in a holding pattern, ever circling, unable to land and unable to fly away.

I worry about what others might think, but if I am going to help anyone, I have to be honest about my feelings. I have done a lot of things by trial and error. Some worked and others made things worse. But painful as it is, I have to own up to my mistakes in this if I can ever hope to comfort anyone else. It's not easy to open up your life and admit to your mistakes, your doubts, your fears, your weaknesses, and your vulnerability.

This is how it was in the beginning. It was how I tried to adjust to our new lives or what I thought of as our "temporary life." I thought if I could just find the right words, actions, or medicine, I could "fix" him. I took this disease on as if it was something I could conquer if I only tried hard enough. There were a lot of mistakes, done with all good intentions, but mistakes nonetheless.

Depression did not arrive with a lot of fanfare. There was no one day we could point to and say, "There, that's the day it all began." I thought that if I could just find that catalyst, that thing that started it all, I could go back and fix it. I could do things different and maybe stop it from ever happening. But no matter how hard I tried, I couldn't find that defining moment, that moment when our lives started to unravel.

It crept up slowly day by day. I didn't even realize what was happening. The changes were little at first, seeming to go back and forth from day to day. I would look back and wonder why I didn't see it coming. There was the constant staring off into space, the going to bed earlier and earlier, the withdrawal from family and friends, the strained conversations or complete lack of interaction, and saddest of all was the loss of enthusiasm for life.

He would struggle to make it to work each day. On the weekends, he slept away most of the day. I struggled to control my temper. I wanted to scream, to yell, even pick a fight, anything to get some sort of reaction from him. It was so frustrating to feel him slipping away and not be able to stop it.

What is going on? I want my life back. I want our life back!

Depression is probably not the first thing that pops in your mind when you begin to notice the changes. It wasn't mine. I knew nothing about depression. It had never been a subject that anyone talked about. I had never known anyone who suffered from it, and I didn't recognize the signs.

I initially thought, *Is he having an affair? Is it another woman and this is just guilt? Can he just not find the words to tell me it is over? Maybe that's why there is no laughter anymore. He's sick and tired of me. That might explain what is going on. I've seen all this before. I've lived it. I've seen that dead, hollow look in someone's eyes. I've felt the lack of participation in everyday life. He is physically there with me, yet mentally he is very far away.*

I jumped to that conclusion for a good reason. I had seen that look for years in my father's eyes. I saw it all the times he was getting ready to walk out again, leaving us behind for someone else. The first time I remember seeing that look was when I was in the second grade. He stood in the doorway poised to leave, staring at me with my suitcase packed ready to go with him. He looked at me with those hollow eyes, shook his head, and walked out, leaving me there struggling to understand what happened. I just knew I wanted to erase that sad, blank look from his eyes.

My dad did come back. But things had changed. The picture of our happy family had shifted. This was the start of the waiting and watching. Would that hollow, disinterested look return? I found my childhood innocence gone. I couldn't stand the silence. I tried to fill the void with talk and jokes. I tried to be perfect. I thought if I could make good grades and keep out of trouble then things would be okay. We could pretend things were back to normal. It didn't last. It couldn't. The look came back. That sense of being present but yet really far away. That sense of guilt that held him there even when all he wanted was to be gone. Once you see that look in someone's eyes, you never forget it. It's a childhood memory that never quite leaves you. It is a look that you never want to see again.

That is the look I first noticed. I started to get that panicky feeling in the pit of my stomach. I was constantly questioning myself. *Is he seeing someone else? Is he thinking about leaving? Is the job of being husband and father too much of a burden?* Old feelings returned and I was scared.

Okay, I can take care of this. I am a grown woman now, not a child. I have been down this road before, but I am stronger now. I started by trying to keep things going smoothly. I tried to handle any fights between the kids. I tried to make sure all the bills were paid on time. I didn't mention money. I didn't point out things that need fixing around the house. I didn't put on the pressure. I thought that maybe if I tried hard enough, I could keep everything under control. I tried to make life at home so pleasant that he wouldn't want to leave. But the doubt was still there. The look had not left his eyes.

As much as I hated myself for doubting, I started looking for clues. I searched his truck for hidden notes. I looked at his cell phone for any messages. I listened to him on the phone to see if I could hear any hidden meanings in his words. I was suspicious of everyone. Was it someone he worked with? Was there someone there that can relate to the pressures of his job in a way that I couldn't? Was there someone there that offered him an escape from the responsibilities that he had in his life with me? I wanted to tell him that I could change. I could make things better. I would try harder. I wanted to beg him just to talk to me, to give me a second chance.

I wanted to run away, far away. I wanted to go far enough to forget the look in his eyes and the sound of despair in his voice. Where could I go? Could I just turn my back and walk away, leaving him to struggle alone? No, I couldn't. My love and my commitments held me there; it was my promise to love him through the good times and the bad.

Finally, I couldn't stand it any longer. I had tried to fix things. I felt all alone, like I was the only one trying to hold our family together. So I confronted him to get things out in the open. He looked confused and completely caught off guard. He told me—swore to me—that everything was okay. There was no other woman. He didn't want to leave me, us.

Things were fine. He told me so, right?

I felt relief, but it didn't last very long. He was still speaking in that low, monotone voice. There were no ups or downs in his speech. The look in his eyes was still there. I wanted to believe so much that everything was okay. I was desperate to believe. But in my heart, I knew things just weren't normal.

Why weren't things brighter now? Why did his eyes still look blank? How come there was no joy, no happiness, no talking? If it wasn't our marriage, then what was this? I tried to smile through my tears. He begged me to believe him and I tried. I pushed the doubts back, pushed them down deep inside me. I hid them even from myself. I hid them so deep that they only surfaced once in a while.

The fears would come back late at night when we were both lying in bed staring at opposite walls. I would curl into myself, feeling alone even though he was so close I could reach out and touch him. But I didn't, I couldn't. I sensed that he had retreated back into himself. He had gone back to that place that I couldn't reach.

If I did manage to fall asleep, I could escape from those feelings. I didn't have to fake a smile. I didn't have to act brave.

Things did not improve with time. He didn't want to go anywhere. We stopped going out to eat. We stopped going to ball games. We stopped attending church. He couldn't make himself leave the house. He was becoming a prisoner in his own mind.

Meanwhile, I was trying even harder to take care of things around the house. I felt all alone in my marriage and alone as a parent.

I wanted to shake him, to slap him, to yell at him. Do anything to get him to snap out of it. Get him to see what a great life he had.

His physical symptoms increased. He had headaches and stomach aches. He went to bed early and would lay there staring off into space. Then one day, he just couldn't go into work. He got physically ill just trying to get dressed. He called in sick. What should I do now? For a split second, the thought crossed my mind that maybe he was faking it. Could someone actually get sick to his stomach by the thought of going to work? I thought, *Aw, come on now, it couldn't be that bad. So you had a few bad days. Nobody just wakes up and says they are ill just thinking about work. Come on, suck it up; you've got a family to support!* That's what I felt like saying, but I didn't. So I told myself that maybe a few days' rest and some stress-free time at home would make him feel better. I watched him carefully, hoping for some sign of improvement. But on the day he was to return to work, he got sick again, physically sick. He was unable to get out the door. He broke down. This was the person I had always leaned on who was falling apart before my very eyes. I had always turned to him for help, but now whom could I turn to? Whom could I ask for help? I didn't want to admit to anyone that my husband was unable to go to work.

I felt completely helpless.

I wanted to hold him. Chase it away for him. Help him. Fix him. I wanted to do anything to make it better. My heart broke for him.

Guilt Guilt Guilt Guilt

I felt guilt that maybe it was my fault. If I had done something, said something, been something different, then maybe it wouldn't have happened.

Nothing was working. I couldn't figure out how to fix it, fix him, fix us. He told me over and over that it was not mine to fix, that it was something he had to deal with. But that wasn't true. He was not in this alone. We were all caught up in the circles that surrounded him. We were all being drawn down into the darkness with him. We were the ones who looked into his eyes and saw the haunted, vacant look staring back at us. His eyes never sparkled with laughter anymore; the laughter was gone. I held onto his hand, the hand that just lay there resting in mine. I would give it a little squeeze, but he was unable to answer back. That was a very lonely feeling.

I wanted to get out, to run away, but I couldn't. I had responsibilities, even more now that he was unable to help me. I had to keep all the balls in the air. I had to keep the family going. I had to keep up some semblance of normalcy to the rest of the world. I cried a lot. I got angry that I couldn't afford the luxury of just zoning out. I was so angry that I would tell him that someone had to work and support us. I would leave those words hanging in the air as I walked out the door. I was acting in complete panic mode. I had to do what I could to take

31

care of the kids. He told me that my unhappiness just added to his guilt.

More guilt . . . now I've managed to make him feel even worse.

He told me that my unhappiness was a constant reflection of his inability to get well. It was a reminder of the effect his illness had on everyone, not just him. But sometimes I felt that he didn't see or recognize the toll it was taking on everyone. It was as if he was in his own world, unable to see the pain in anyone's eyes other than his own.

When people called, he wouldn't answer. Friends would ask us over; he wouldn't go. I made excuses for him. Excuses like he wasn't home, he just fell asleep, he wasn't feeling well, he was just so tired, and so on and so on. I couldn't tell them the truth, so I lied. I couldn't tell them that he wouldn't go anywhere, not even to work. He would just sit and stare into space. I ran out of excuses. How could I explain his behavior to someone on the outside? I had no explanation for it. I didn't think they would understand. How could they when I didn't even understand it myself? Eventually, they would quit calling and quit asking us to go out. I felt they were unsure of what was going on, but they were tired of being turned down every time. I actually felt relieved that I didn't have to come up with excuses anymore.

A little part of me wished someone would step in and ask what was wrong. I wished someone else would have come over to help me figure out what was going on. Couldn't anyone see my pain, my confusion? But I didn't push it. I had been making excuses too long. I even repeated those same excuses to myself over and over. Now I wonder just who was I trying harder to convince, me or them?

Loneliness, alone, so alone

I wanted to talk to him. He was my best friend, the one person I could share everything with. But I couldn't. I held it all in.

Breaking point . . .

I called his primary doctor who happened to be a family friend. I had to talk to someone. He had known us for a long time. He knew the man my husband once was, a man who had been self-assured, confident in his decisions, a take-charge kind of guy. I felt that he would understand how concerned we were over the changes that were happening. I explained how he had been acting. I let it all come pouring out. It was a relief to finally tell someone, to admit how scared I was for him.

It felt so good to finally say the words out loud. But now they were out there, and I couldn't take them back or make them go away; I would have to face what was happening, whatever it was. His first question was, "Is he home alone and do you think he would do anything to himself?" Wait a minute; what was he talking about? I hadn't ever let that thought enter my mind. I suddenly couldn't stop shaking. I was scared beyond words. I felt like the ground had just opened up beneath me.

He told me to stay there with him and to make sure there was nothing there that he could harm himself with. Was this really happening? It seemed surreal. It

33

seemed like I had suddenly stepped into a movie. This wasn't my life. He asked if I could get him to come to the office, but I confessed that I couldn't get him to leave the house at all. Our doctor said he would come by the house and talk to us both.

Calling the doctor had to be one of the most frightening things I had ever done in my whole life. I was afraid that I had opened Pandora's box and things would never be the same again. A million thoughts ran through my head. Would he need to be admitted to the hospital? What if I had waited too long to ask for help? Why hadn't I reached out to someone sooner? What was I going to tell the kids when they got home from school? What would happen to us?

Waiting for the doctor to arrive had to be one of the longest thirty-minute waits I ever experienced. He sat down and talked to us both. Our answers seemed to confirm what he had originally thought—depression. Scary images began to flash through my mind, frightening images like the ones from movies I had seen and books I had read. He explained the chemical imbalance in the brain that could cause depression. He even drew us a picture; I guess we were looking pretty shell shocked. He talked about trying medicines for the time being and following up with future appointments. We were very quiet, trying to take it all in.

I felt scared but strengthened a little. This thing had a name. It had happened before. Other people had been where we were. There were treatments. My husband slowly nodded his head. He finally felt as if these feelings he'd been having had been verified. A glimmer of hope returned. It wasn't much, but at last, we felt as if we had something to hold on to.

It was an illness, not a choice. But still, depression is often misunderstood. I didn't realize it until I lived it. I don't think anyone can truly sympathize with you unless they have been through it also.

I grabbed onto anything I could find about this illness like a drowning woman to a life preserver. I wanted to know what could cause it, what different medicines there were to treat it, and the different ideas for and against pills. I searched the Internet for any information I could find. I was determined to learn what I could about it and how to fight it. We made an appointment with our doctor again and with a psychologist. We were taking steps. The war had begun—the war of reclaiming our life together.

I found lots of books about depression, but they all seemed to relate to the person actually suffering from the illness. Where were the books for ones who were going through it with them? Where was our help, our books? We were expected to be strong. We were expected to hold everything together and give them time to concentrate on getting well. We were expected to go on living our lives, keeping things going, act like things were normal, and put on a brave front for the world.

My husband and I suffered in silence. We got up each day and put on a smile, but inside I could feel myself sinking, drowning. Questions would run through my mind constantly. *Would our life ever be the same again? Where was the hope? How long could I keep this up?* I told myself that things would get better, of course they would. But a small part of me was scared to death that this was our new normal.

Life kept going on all around us, but I felt strangely removed from it all. I was so caught up in my own net of fear and hurt that I felt angry with everyone else. I was jealous of the couple in front of me holding hands. I actually hurt when I heard people discussing weekend plans in front of me. I would leave places in tears, unable to see other people living their normal lives.

He began to take an antidepressant. They said it could take up to two weeks for us to see if this first medicine would work. I anxiously watched him for any sign of improvement. The first few days he seemed better, but before the next week had gone by, we knew this one wasn't working. So we went back to the doctor and tried another medicine. What I had hoped was a quick cure was turning into a waiting game. He started the next medicine and again I waited and watched. Was this one going to work? We realized that he might have to go through several medicines and even two at the same time to get the balance just right. It was something, a start anyway.

I desperately wanted, needed, to talk to someone, anyone. But at the same time, I wanted to protect him. I wanted to shield him from any more hurt. I didn't want anyone to lose respect for him. At the time he was diagnosed, I had never known anyone who suffered from a mental illness. Who should I tell? Who could I trust? How much should I tell them? Would people be afraid to be around us? Would they understand or would they withdraw as if it was contagious? Would they let their kids still come over to play? Some would, some wouldn't. I wasn't able to predict how anyone would react, and I couldn't control it.

Most people don't know what to say when faced with someone's illness. If you weren't the one living with it, how would you react? Don't focus on them. Move on, forgive, and focus your energy on the important things.

Sometimes I felt like most of my friends had deserted me. I felt like I had no one to talk to. No one understood what I was going through. I felt selfish to be worrying about myself; I should be focused on the one who was sick. I couldn't explain it to anyone. You had to live it to understand it, and it was not something I would wish on anyone.

But no, not all would fall away. Some friends would show up when things seemed hopeless and I felt lost. They would give me the boost I needed to keep going. They would give me a shoulder to cry on. There was the invitation for a cup of coffee, an unexpected card in the mail, an offer of babysitting, or sometimes just a smile. Little gestures became much more meaningful. Sometimes that's the best thing anyone can do—just be there. I wanted to remember how those small gestures of kindness made me feel so that I could share them with others in need later.

Have others felt like this or am I the only one?

Scared

I remember being too scared to leave the house, afraid of what could happen, but not being able to bear it another minute. I had to get away, even for just a minute. I would look around the house, making sure the knives were not out on the counter and that the medicines were all put up. Yes, it felt silly, ridiculous even, but I couldn't help myself. Even though he told me that he was not even thinking that, I couldn't help but feel scared.

It was around this time that he started seeing a psychologist. It was very hard to get him to go to his appointments. Sometimes I drove him and waited outside. Sometimes I used a guilt trip and said, "Do it for me, us, the kids." I would try anything to get him in there and talking. I also attended some sessions. These were eye openers for us both. I learned the strain he had been under trying to hold it all together, not wanting to seem weak. He got to hear how I was feeling in a nonconfrontational way. We attended joint sessions and solo ones.

Our psychologist told me that if I wanted to go out, I should ask him to go with me but not press the issue. If he didn't want to go, then I should just go on without him. That was easier said than done. Going out for ice cream or a ride is kind of lonely and sad knowing that he was sitting at home or maybe just had given up already and gone on to bed. I tried very hard to go, but I have to admit that it wasn't much fun.

There was the desire to escape, even if only in a physical sense. Driving, driving. Not wanting to go home, but knowing I had to pick it up and try to carry on. I was afraid of what I would come home to. Was he depressed enough to do something desperate? He said no, but would he tell me if he was?

I tried to hide the panic from him, from the kids, and everyone else. I kept telling everyone that he was just tired, and I tried to convince myself of that also.

I went to work, because we needed the money, but I also needed to get away from all of it for a little while. I would then rush to get home before the kids did, afraid of what they might find. Every time I opened the door, I would hold my breath, scared for a second, not knowing what I might see.

He still couldn't go to work; he just couldn't make himself go. He had to take short-term disability. In my mind I screamed, *What will we do? How will we pay the bills? How will we get by? Go to work, go to work, I'm scared, I'm terrified, tell me what I should do!* I felt more alone than I had ever been. I felt abandoned. But on the outside, I nodded and said, "Take some time off, feel better, get better." All the while, I tried to keep the panic from my voice.

Desperate

I was even more desperate for someone to talk to, to have a conversation with. I tried to talk to the kids. Well, teenagers are not known for their desire to have long, meaningful conversations with their parents. Besides, I felt guilty for putting this on them, so I continued to suffer in relative silence.

I searched my children's eyes. Would they inherit this illness? Would I recognize it in time and catch it before it consumed them? I felt that I had already failed my husband, that I didn't recognize it quickly enough get him help before it went so far. So I watched them, listened to them, talked to them, still trying in vain to keep things looking and feeling normal. I hated for them to see their dad so lost, so unsure, so I kept them moving. I took them to friends' houses—smoke and mirrors— "Pay no attention to the silent man . . . everything is fine."

One unexpected good thing did come out of this. With their dad unable to participate very much in their day-to-day lives, I stepped in. We were able to get out by ourselves, away from the stress at home. I taught both kids to drive, which was a challenge, but it was one-on-one time that I will always treasure. However, he and the kids missed out on what is usually a rite of passage shared between father and child. I felt so bad for the kids and angry with him. I felt that he should have tried harder to connect with them. I still feel bad for what all of them missed out on, but instead of blaming him, I am trying to look at it as a special time that was shared between me and the kids.

I hope, I pray

I couldn't talk to his mom. She was dealing with enough, so I hid it, or tried to. I made excuses for him. I tried to be behind the scenes picking up the slack, doing the things his mom needed him to do. I tried to fill the void before it was noticed. But I couldn't help but wonder, *How can she not see this? Can't she read it in his eyes, see it in his face?* Maybe not. He tried to hide it when he was around her, to spare himself the questions. To say it out loud would make it real. If it was not spoken of, maybe it was not really true.

So I talked, told jokes, tried to coax out a laugh, a smile, any response and eventually giving up, but knowing I'd be back to try again. Oh how I wanted to turn my back, pick up my life, and go on. I wanted to be able to laugh and feel something other than this. But each time, I came back to try again.

Some days I wanted him to hear me crying, see my red eyes. I wanted him to feel bad. I wanted to make him see what he was doing to me, to us. I wanted to say to him, **"Stop it! Stop it now! I can't take it anymore.**

Only you can stop it. Try harder please! Come back, come back to us!"

I am embarrassed and sorry to say that I *did* try that; I was willing to try anything. It didn't do any good. It just seemed to make him feel worse and that did not help anyone. But sometimes my emotions got the best of me. I would hold it in as long as I could. I would force the smiles, talk, make conversation, and act normal. Then something inside me would break. Maybe I would hear a song, maybe he would say he was sorry he couldn't come back, and the dam that I had worked so hard to build up would break. The tears would come, those hot, sudden floods of tears that never seemed to stop. Tears for him, for me, for the couple we once were, for all we'd shared, for all we'd missed, and for the fear that it was all lost. He would tell me that he was trying. He would fake a smile. He would take my hand. It was all forced; I knew it and he knew it. But I loved him for trying, knowing what the effort cost him. And once again, I tried to be the strong one. I had to be. I would gather up my emotions and put them away in a box, only to be brought out when I was alone.

Many days, I just couldn't go on. I would cry all the way to work. I would have to pull the car over because I was crying so hard. At work, I would go in the bathroom and cry, silent, hot tears of defeat, sadness, and hopelessness.

I found myself crying when the commercials for antidepressants came on TV. I knew so well just how those people felt, and it made me feel even sadder. I wanted to turn them off, but something made me watch them over and over. I would also listen to sad songs. Maybe it was because in some small way they reflected what we were going through. I hoped that eventually I wouldn't have any tears left to cry.

To hope

Some days, I would try to wake up and go about as if things were normal. I put my fears aside for a day, ignored things, and just lived. The days seemed to stretch endlessly, one day fading seamlessly into the next. I would wake up only to have reality come crashing back down on me. I would pick up my worries and put them back on like I would an old pair of shoes, not because they were comfortable but because they were the only pair I owned. I was always hesitant of what the new day would bring.

One day I asked myself, *When was the last time you smiled, laughed, felt joy, or felt optimism?* I couldn't remember! Was this how he felt? Is this how it happened, just one day you wake up and realize that you couldn't face it all again? You were just too tired to make the effort. Then the questions and guilt would flood in. How would we survive if we were both like this? Who would pick up the pieces of our lives?

A never-ceasing worry

"But I called on your name, Lord, from deep within the pit."
(Lamentations 3:55)

EVER-WIDENING CIRCLES

The Other Side

I had to get help for me.

I realized that I had to talk to someone not connected to our family. I didn't want anyone to think badly about him. I didn't want them to look at him differently, but I needed help. Luckily, I had a doctor's appointment coming up, and I forced myself to go. When my doctor asked me how I had been, it all came pouring out, like a dam that had broken loose. All the tears, the fears, and the guilt were released. My doctor didn't judge, and she didn't look horrified. She just listened to me. I was finally able to express my feelings without the pressure of having to be "strong." It was like a weight had been lifted off my shoulders.

Just opening up to someone who had no connection to the depressed person left me free to say how I really felt. Yes, I felt ashamed as I spilled all the hurt, confusion, and anger that I had felt, but I also felt a huge relief to get it out into the open. Those emotions had been strangling me, so it was great to actually say it all out loud without fear of being judged. This was a huge boost to me. I felt that I could go on; I felt stronger. She prescribed an antidepressant, and I hesitated but decided that if she thought I needed it, then I would give it a try.

I began to open up to other people and ask the people I trusted what they saw. At first, some thought that he was just trying to get out of doing something. That it was just an excuse. But the longer it went on, they saw the difference in me also. I kept everyone away from him; not too many people made it through me to get to him. I ran interference. I'd like to come off sounding noble and steadfast, standing strong, protecting my family. That's what I wanted to be, what I wanted everyone to see me as, and sometimes I actually pulled it off. My family and friends thought I was handling it, taking care of things like I always have. Some said they never really understood how bad it was because they never talked with him or saw him. I didn't know if I was doing the right thing or not, I was just trying to hold it all together. He was uncomfortable around people so I just kept everyone away. <u>Period.</u>

Parallel feelings

At times, we all feel alone. Everyone wants to ease a loved one's pain; I have been on that other side. I have been the one everyone tiptoes around, watching, unsure of what to do or say. Neither side is ideal to be on. When you are faced with an illness, you feel alone and isolated, even though everyone is there beside you. You feel scared, unsure of your future, even while everyone reassures you that things will be okay. You watch everyone dance around you. They try so hard to cheer you up. You smile and nod, but inside you know that you are hanging on by a thread. You don't want to hurt them, but sometimes you just want to shout at them, "I'm scared; I don't know if everything will be okay!" But you don't. They are trying so hard, and you can't hurt them. You can't let them see. Sometimes you even convince yourself that you can handle this.

You see, I have had my turn at being strong for the people I love. At age thirty-five, I had a kidney removed due to cancer, followed by a partial removal of my thyroid, a hysterectomy, a suspicious cyst in my breast, and skin cancer that left a 3" x 3" scar on top of my head. But each of these was something that could be seen on an x-ray or CT scan, something that could be operated on and removed. I was able to say, okay, there it is, that's what wrong; let's get it out. Somehow in my mind, that made it a little easier to deal with.

Now you can see that both sides have similar wants and needs. Both want to be reassured by the other that everything will be okay, that things will return to normal. Each side comforts the other. What you feel, no matter which side of this you are on, is all right. It's normal. We are all scared. We are all human.

Seasons

"For everything there is a season, a time for every activity under heaven. A time to be born and a time to die. A time to plant and a time to harvest. A time to kill and a time to heal. A time to tear down and a time to build up. A time to cry and a time to laugh. A time to grieve and a time to dance" (Ecclesiastes 3:1–4).

I began to measure the days of our lives as seasons. My "summer" husband is fun, outgoing, and entertaining. He laughs, talks, cooks . . . we communicate. It is like the old days before depression became a part of our lives. Maybe a little sweeter because I now know that like all seasons, it will begin to fade and another season will take its place.

Our "winter" season is a different story. In August, I notice less people come over; the weekends are spent more in front of the TV. The word "later" starts creeping in more and more of our conversations. In October, the leaves change and so does the pattern of our lives. In November, the trees become bare. Each day feels the same. I feel myself turning gray just like the skies and the trees around me. December was once my favorite month, with the hustle and bustle and Christmas wishes. Now he wishes he could skip this month and avoid the holidays completely. He quits socializing, and he even stops going to church. I go out, buy all the presents, and address the cards, but I feel so alone. I see other families out celebrating the season, and I feel like crying and screaming all at the same time.

I keep telling myself that another spring is just around the corner. Soon the trees will begin to bud, and my summer husband will return. I just have to hold on a little longer, be patient.

Hang on!

Over ten years have passed since that day the doctor came to our house and we began this journey that has occupied such a part of our lives. Where did all that time go?

I feel like the years have gone by in a fog, a haze of confusion, desperation, anger, and sadness. Sometimes I think back and think it must all have been a bad dream.

What's so weird is that there are good days in the midst of the bad. There are days when things seem almost normal. He tells me that things are better. But by the next morning, I can tell by the way he moves that it is back. I sense the switch being turned off, and his desire to get out of bed and participate in life disappears again.

In the morning when the alarm goes off, I hold my breath to see if he is going to get up to go to work. I try not to ask, but I can't help myself. I turn on the TV, turn on the lights, go make coffee, and finally I just have to ask. I am dreading the answer, but I need to know.

Every time this happens, it kills a little part of me. I don't say this for anyone to feel sorry for me; I am just stating a fact. I feel a little bit of myself wither and die. My shoulders sag from the weight of another bout with this disease. My mouth tires from forcing the smiles, and my eyes burn from holding back the tears. I may grow weaker each time, but I don't give up; he needs me.

Can I take this again? Can I make it through another one? Do I have the strength, the will, and the desire to face this one? I ask myself those questions each and every time, and every time it gets harder and harder to know the answer. I worry that one day I will have had enough and give up on him and us. I also worry that he might give up on himself.

Trying it alone

One day, he decided to take himself off his medicine. He did it the right way by checking with his primary doctor. He weaned himself off slowly.

I didn't quite figure it out until we were moving our youngest child home from the dorm at the end of freshman year. I noticed that things didn't seem quite right, and I couldn't figure out what was wrong. Finally, back at the hotel, I came right out and asked him what was wrong. He then told me about taking himself off his antidepressant medicine. I was so angry. He said that it was his decision, not mine. But that didn't change the fact that he forgot to check with me, the other person living with this. I felt betrayed because he didn't consult me on such a big decision. After all we had been through, *I* had been through, and he would do this?

After much discussion—arguing—he started back taking his medicine slowly. Things started to return to what was now our new normal. Summertime, grilling, everything seemed all right.

Then the day came when we loaded up the trailer and moved the youngest back again to college and a new apartment. We had a three hundred-mile trip in front of us and at mile marker 8, he stared straight ahead and said he felt anxious and didn't know why. *Oh no, not now! Please not now!* But depression doesn't seem to respect anyone's timetable.

I tried to come up with all kinds of logical reasons like the youngest child moving out on his own, worries about him paying for college, pulling a trailer across the state, etc. But he said no, none of those things were really bothering him any more than usual.

We unloaded the trailer and headed to the hotel. The next morning, he grew quieter and more withdrawn. I tried to fill the morning with jokes and hoped that the kids would not notice how their father was acting. The day seemed to grow darker. By two o'clock that afternoon, he was not talking at all. He yelled, "It's time to go, NOW!" He didn't want to talk about it. It was a long trip home. I have heard people say that they cried all the way home, and I always thought that seemed a little exaggerated. Not so. I know now that it can happen. I cried for him and for me. I was in shock. This depression had hit in what seemed like the space of twenty-four hours. I had never seen anything like it and even after all these years, sometimes I still feel totally unprepared.

He sank just like that stone thrown into the pond. It was one of the quickest onsets we had experienced. I could see myself sliding into the darkness with him. It was even easier to do now because the kids were off to college, and it was just him and me at home.

During the week, I would find myself trying to get home before he did. I think maybe it was just to be able to relax and let my shoulders rest from the burden I seemed to carry everywhere I went.

Time began to pass so slowly, each day slipping into the next. We both grew quieter. Winter had come very early that year.

At this same time, my stepdad had been diagnosed with cancer. He had to spend a lot of time in and out of the hospital and each time I went to visit him, I went alone. The feelings from when my father-in-law had been diagnosed with cancer and passed away years ago came back to the surface again and as before, we seemed to be unable to lean on each other for comfort. When my father-in-law passed away, I was left alone to grieve and tell our children. When my stepdad passed away at the end of November, I was again left alone to deal with my grief. My husband tried to be there, but I began to question if I could ever count on him again. We both dealt with our grief separately. Again, he was unable to fight through his depression to see my pain. As what happens sometimes when a death occurs, my immediate family became estranged. I felt the loneliness crushing me.

He withdrew more into himself, and I felt abandoned once again. I felt like I was being drawn in again to the deep, dark abyss. I would spend hours just sitting parked at a local drive-in restaurant. I would just sit and cry for everything I had lost. Just sit in my car and cry. Even the carhops began to recognize me and would just nod as they went by, not quite making eye contact.

I would go to church and sit next to him, together, yet miles apart. If we went out, I did all the talking. I would try to engage him in conversation, but he would just stare off into space. Eventually, I just quit trying.

I would drive around town and listen to Christian radio. How did they know which song to play, the exact one that I needed right then? At church, every sermon seemed to be written for me. I felt as if God was trying so hard to reach me, but I wasn't capable of reaching out to take His hand.

My breaking point

I remember the night I lost it. I realized that he was the one with depression, yet I was the one who thought about ending my life, unable to face this again. I just didn't feel that I could go through it again.

Hopelessness

I began looking for ways to put an end to it all. I would drive to work and think about ways to do it. I looked at running off a bridge, but then I figured my car would probably float. I looked at running my car into a tree, but it would probably bounce off. And yes, I know it sounds silly but those ridiculous excuses gave me pause enough to think better of it. It's ironic isn't it? He was the one with depression, and I was the one thinking about suicide. I am ashamed to admit that those were my thoughts, but it is the truth. I knew I needed help. So I called for help, outside help, professional help. Help for just me this time. I had lost all my joy, my happiness. The light felt like it had left me, and I could only see darkness. I was so tired of fighting, tired of watching, waiting. I started driving with a picture of my kids on the dash of my car to remind me of what I had to live for, to continue fighting for.

I went to see a therapist the next day. We discussed my feelings of sadness, hopelessness, and abandonment. I started going every week and every week she asked and listened. She pointed out that perhaps I was grieving. Naturally. I was grieving the loss of my stepdad and the members of my family that were lost as well. She asked me if I had ever considered that maybe I was grieving the loss of my marriage, companionship, and trust in the man I had married.

We began to look at the five stages of grief:

1. Denial—Refusing to accept the reality of my life now
2. Anger—I was definitely mad over how my life had changed, and felt like it was completely out of my control.

3. Bargaining—If I just try harder, I know I can fix things, make him better.
4. Depression—The realization that things will never change. Each year is just a repeat of the last.
5. Acceptance—I had to decide if I was willing to continue in this pattern or break it off and step out alone.

I began to see how I had been slowly following these stages over the past years. With every new bout of depression, I pulled a little further away.

Do you recognize any of those behaviors in you?

It was a real wake-up call for me. I had no idea that I could mourn the loss of a marriage while I was still in the middle of it. I saw that I had been slowly experiencing those five stages of grief over the span of ten years. I had experienced feelings of loss of friendship, companionship, trust, and the feeling of having someone there for me. During those depressive episodes, a small part of our marriage had died without either one of us actually being aware of it.

I attended a grief survivor's group one evening. I felt self-conscious about attending; my grief seemed trivial compared to theirs. But they were so kind, compassionate, and strong, and I learned so much. I realized that my grief was real, and it was a comfort to acknowledge it and put it in perspective.

That holiday season I would see couples and families out shopping together and my anger and sadness would overwhelm me. I would leave the stores in tears. I mourned what I had lost and feared I would never have it again.

Tired . . .

I was physically and mentally exhausted. I was worn out. I didn't know what to do. Could we get our marriage back? Had I exhausted so much energy grieving its loss that I couldn't even see myself getting back into it? Did I even want to risk going through that again, risking what little was left of me to pursue that relationship again? I wrestled with my decision; it was not an easy one to make. We had been together for thirty-three years. The last ten years had not been so much a marriage as it had been two people on the edge, waiting for a good day, week, month, or the beginning of another dark season. Why did I hesitate? This was my chance to live again, free from all the strain.

A different season . . .

This year's season took a different path. He shared this story with me when I woke up one morning after the kids had gone back to school after Christmas break.

One night while I was still asleep, he began to pray. He asked God for help. He asked God to help him help me, to help him be a better husband, and to help him be a better father and stand beside his family. And he asked to be delivered from depression. He was tired of dealing with it all and needed God's help. He said they fought, he yelled, and he came very close to turning his back on God, but he continued to pray. At one point, he felt the hands of God on his shoulders and received a comfort that he hadn't known since his dad had died.

He shared this with me the next day, and I was happy for him but to be honest, I was a little bit skeptical. I know God performs many miracles, but due to the many ups and downs of this illness, I hesitated to jump right in. I told him I was going to stay back and observe him. To me, his actions would speak louder than his words. He began to open up to other people, telling them of his battle with depression and how God had healed him. He was able to comfort several people who were going through similar battles. It was the first time I had heard him tell anyone that he had depression. It appeared that things were different this time.

However, this new feeling seemed to take over everything in his life. He could not stop talking; he talked every waking moment. He posted to Facebook continuously. He had an opinion about everything and everybody, and if you *did* get a word in edgewise, he disagreed with it. It became impossible to go out to dinner with him. He would get up in everyone's face, up so close that you could see their discomfort. He was even asked to leave a restaurant because they felt he was too overly talkative with a server, and they were uncomfortable. I felt so sad that he was completely oblivious to his behavior. None of this was like him; this was completely out of character for him. He had never been like this before. This was definitely not normal; it wasn't even the "new" normal we had had the last several years. He would have bursts of anger, seemingly coming out of nowhere. I continued to withdraw from it all. His behavior was startling. He spent money on things we really did not need, and they were not joint decisions; they were things he had decided we needed. He was drinking black coffee all the time and not eating. He lost a lot of weight. He was sleeping very little, getting up after a few hours, and getting on the computer. He became more involved with church, which was not a bad thing, but he seemed unable to limit his involvement. He was donating money to many causes and wanted to donate even more. He read the Bible constantly and while that was also a good thing, he would tell me repeatedly how sad it was that I was not as secure in my faith as he was. He would get angry when I said I thought he might be going overboard in all these things. He would tell me that maybe one day I would be able to feel like he did. He constantly told me that he was disappointed in me and that I hurt his feelings because he had poured out his heart to me and I still didn't trust him.

I became very concerned about him. The angry outbursts, the inappropriate conversations with friends and strangers . . . it all just didn't feel right. He would send random texts to our kids and others. He seemed almost manic. I actually became scared for him. At times, I became frightened that I might be physically harmed. He did not seem right. I was so confused and so worried. He also began to drink excessively. He had always had a few beers after work or early afternoon on the weekends to "relax," but a few soon turned into more and more. I admit that at first I joined him in drinking. I guess I hoped it would numb the hurts and confusion. But when the buzz wore off, those hurts were still there. The alcohol only shoved them down for a little while. They were always just under the surface waiting to appear. I knew that the answer I was searching for could not be found in a bottle. He didn't understand why I was no longer willing to join him every afternoon in a drink. My explanation didn't seem to make sense to him. I began to count the bottles in the refrigerator every afternoon so I could judge when he was drinking more. He could not understand that the alcohol just sent him into a deeper, sadder place. I began to just avoid him when he would drink. I couldn't bear to see him slur his words or stumble as he walked. When I would point out that I thought he was drinking too much, he would become angry and say that that was the only way he could relax and I needed to get off his back about it. I began to consider attending Alcoholics Anonymous meetings just so I could try to understand and maybe make some sense out of what he was going through.

I found out that he had, again, taken himself off his medication. I felt betrayed once again for not being consulted over something that affects me too. I began to look up information on manic depression and bipolar disorder. He seemed to have many of the symptoms: lots of energy with only a few hours' sleep, talking incessantly and nervously, spending without thinking ahead, hostility, irritability, overzealous religious involvement, impulsiveness, etc. Maybe this wasn't just depression; maybe there was an underlying reason that we hadn't thought of or recognized before. It was time to start over.

The highs are like a balloon climbing higher and higher. Eventually, you notice that it has quit rising and is slowly coming down to the ground. The question is, will it land gently or crash and bust? I had to ask myself if I was willing to be there to pick up the pieces when it did.

One of the things I came to realize was that I could no longer hold on to that balloon and take that ride with him. The highs and the lows were taking too great a toll on me. It became harder and harder for me to recover from these, and I was afraid that after too many more of them I would not come back. My therapist pointed out that instead of trying to go on those up and down rides, I should try to keep my feet on the ground and maintain a steady influence for the children and us. I did not have to get on every roller coaster. It was okay for me to sit out a few rides. I just needed to be there when the ride was over to see that everyone got off safely.

I did a lot of soul searching, a lot. I suggested marriage counseling to him. He emphatically said no. He said that I was the only one who seemed to have a problem with the way he was acting. When the time came for our appointment, I said I would go by myself to see if there was anything left to save. I couldn't give up without making sure. He did decide to go and wound up talking through the entire appointment. I just sat there feeling small, petty, and even stupid for taking it this far. I spent a lot of time wishing on one hand, that I had never started this journey and on the other hand, grateful for a second chance at a life. I hoped that this time we would get it right. I would leave every session and ride around by myself just soul searching. Was I the one who was all wrong in this? I felt even more confused.

I would love to say that during therapy I discovered that I had done everything right. But no, that is far from the truth! While I did everything with the best intentions, I began to see the many errors I had made throughout the years. And yes, it is hard to admit to this when all along I thought the underlying problem was all his. But we all need to learn that there are two sides to every story, and I have to own up to my part in this.

I also found that I had allowed myself to fall into a "yes" pattern. If he was convinced it would make him happy, then I was willing to say yes, anything to make him smile. At first, it was easy for me if it brought a smile to his face and for a while, he actually seemed happier. Soon, a pattern began to emerge; the more I said yes, the less it kept him happy and the more resentful I became. In spending money and making plans, it was just easier to smile and go along. I found myself saying yes even if it went against my better judgment because it was just easier.

After years of this resentment building up, I just couldn't stand it any longer. During therapy, I realized that by agreeing with him, I had isolated him from any confrontation. All of my resentment kept building up, and I reached the point where I could no longer hold it back. My resentment came out in angry bursts. I wanted to assert my wants and needs. I was so tired of everything being slanted toward his "happiness" that I wanted things to be about me for a change. I started to confront him about ideas that I didn't agree with. It was tense. I was changing a long pattern that we had both become accustomed to, and it wasn't easy. Many times, I just wanted to give in and go back to those old patterns, but time had already proven that that was not the answer. We are still working on that part of it. He gets resentful when I say I don't agree, but I feel more like myself now, more like a person in my own right. I am not just riding the waves of depression. I am trying to swim to shore.

Now here is where all my work at protecting him in the past came back, and it proved to be a mistake.

People told me how concerned they were for him and his erratic behavior, but I tried to shield him. I felt that if I could make him see how he was behaving, without other people telling him, it would soften it somehow and not hurt so much. I was still protecting him, but doing neither one of us any favors. My therapist helped me to understand that by shielding him, he never had to face any consequences of his actions. I started suggesting that the kids talk to their dad directly; I could no longer be the go-between.

Remember when I said earlier that I had to put all my emotions in a box only to be taken out when I was alone? Again, wrong thing to do! Those pesky emotions got sick of being kept in that box and the effort of keeping them there began to take all my energy. Sadness began to slip out. Anger and resentment followed close behind.

Are you starting to see a pattern here? This journey has been mostly trial and error, and through those errors, I began a journey that ultimately led back to discovering who I really am.

I discovered that I felt abandoned by him. I felt that he had already checked out of our marriage even though physically he was still there. Those old feelings from my father walking out all those years ago resurfaced, threatening to drown me again in waves of unworthiness. During all those years of my husband pulling away, I finally recognized that I had fallen back on old habits learned in childhood. *Maybe if I am really good, take care of everything, and don't cause any trouble, everything will stay the same and no one will go away.* It's a hard lesson to learn; it didn't work then, and it wasn't working now. No matter what I did or had done, it would not alter the reality of my life.

All the tap dancing in the world would not make anyone stay if they didn't want to.

I began to realize that he had actually left me years ago, and I had helped him do it! By me trying to smooth things out, keep conflict from him, and handle things by myself, I had enabled him to withdraw from life. You better believe it took a lot of convincing to get me to see the truth in that statement! So, am I saying that all that scrambling to hold things together was actually the wrong thing? Not wrong exactly, but perhaps by keeping all conflict from him, he became accustomed to the "no conflict zone" and was never even aware of the lengths I went to shield him. Maybe I did too good of a job!

Anger

I also realized that I had been holding on to so much anger. Anger over shouldering all the daily responsibilities, anger over playing go-between for him and the children, and mostly anger that he hadn't even noticed me doing all those things!

What an awakening for me. Instead of holding all the stress of everyday living to myself, I could have, *should* have been involving him. He was completely unaware of all the things I had been doing behind the scenes. I should have let him take responsibility for his own happiness. It was not my job or my responsibility to fix him. He needed to learn how to "fix" himself. I had to give up pushing him to get better.

One day, I realized that I was the one doing all the therapy sessions, attending all the meetings, doing all the reading, and taking all the steps! What was he doing now to change things? Nothing, at least nothing that I could see. While each book, each session, and each meeting drew me closer to finding me, it did not change him. Instead of doing all these things to help him, they had actually been helping me, and that is a great thing! I am the only one I can change anyway so instead of looking at each thing as how this can benefit us, I began to see how it could benefit my life and make me stronger. I began to take charge of my life and make decisions for me. If I was going to be alone in this, then I needed to learn how to take care of me. I began to look at things that brought me happiness, peace, and contentment. I began to spend time thinking about my life and what I wanted to do with it. I wanted to start thinking of the future again and not just exist from day to day. I wanted to stop this circling and land that plane at last! I realized I didn't have to decide right away where we were going as a couple. It was okay to take time to rediscover me and see where that would take me. I finally felt myself able to take a deep breath and look ahead. I couldn't see a clear path, but as Martin Luther King Jr. said, "Faith is taking the first step, even when you can't see the whole staircase." It was a beginning for me, one I hadn't allowed myself to think of in a long, long time.

I think he saw that we were not able to continue as we had been. I could not continue to go on in this pattern forever. Something had to change other than just me if our marriage was to continue. He realized that he needed more therapy just for him.

Sometimes all you can do is to be there, hold their hand, and let your love, strength, and faith hold you both up.

Each life touches another . . .
and another . . .

"Rise during the night and cry out. Pour out your hearts
like water to the Lord. Lift up your hands to him in
prayer, pleading for your children . . ."
(Lamentations 2:19)

CIRCLES WITHIN CIRCLES

A Mother's Worry

I worry about our children. Like I mentioned earlier, you are constantly watching them, trying to read their thoughts. I don't want to push, but I try my best to talk to them about stress and how to handle it.

When this all started, one of our children was a teenager, preparing to step out into the world, busy with all the thoughts and emotions that go along with becoming an adult. She was immersed in her grown-up world, seemingly oblivious to what was going on at home and keeping busy in order to avoid the uneasy feeling that occupied our home. She was busy getting ready to go to college, soon to be away from all this. Far removed from the day-to-day things that make one uneasy, never sure what mood everyone will be in.

Then the bigger worries began. What if something happens at college? Away from home, who would watch for the signs, read the look in her eyes? I called and checked in to see how she sounded. I tried to read between the lines. A break up with her "true love," a bad grade on an exam, or running low on money, all the many things that happen in a young adult's life—could this bring on depression? I called just to listen to her voice.

Time passed, and I even began to relax a little. But then one day I got a phone call and I heard it in her voice, the long breath taken before speaking. I had to sit down because my knees were shaking so badly. She felt overwhelmed, anxious, unable to sleep, and unable to eat. She couldn't even stay on the phone. "Mom, I just can't talk right now. I'll call you later. I love you." CLICK. Just like that, she hung up.

Panic overwhelmed me. I almost fell to the floor. After you've been through it once, the possibility of facing it again, long distance, is overwhelming. I began praying for the wisdom to know how to handle it. My first thought was to get in the car and drive straight there.

I suddenly got a glimpse of what my mother-in-law must have felt these past years, a desire to fix everything but not sure how to go about it. Do I just ignore it, talk upbeat, and hope it goes away? No, I know that doesn't work.

We didn't hear anything for several days. Her friend called, worried, and told us that she was acting withdrawn, didn't want to go out, and just stayed in her room until it was time to go to work. When I called, she told me that there was no joy and no reason for anything. I gave her a number to call, someone she could talk to that was there to listen. She agreed to call.

I put the phone down slowly and began to pray. I prayed a lot, asking God to give both of us strength, guidance, and faith. I asked others to pray for us as well.

"When you walk, their counsel will lead you. When you sleep, they will protect you. When you wake up, they will advise you" (Proverbs 6:22).

Our youngest child spent more time at home with his dad's depression, too young to go out with friends, too young to get away and just be a kid. I would ask friends with kids the same age to have him over to play as often as possible. I wanted to give him a chance to live as normal a life as possible in the midst of all this. My son watched his dad a lot and realized that things had changed drastically. I think the hardest thing was trying to explain why Dad could not take part in our lives. He realized then that his dad was no longer the dad he had once known.

Soon, it was his turn for college. I tried to think of all the things I needed to say before leaving that dorm room, but the excitement of being on his own was so contagious that I tried to keep my anxieties from dampening those feelings. I thought back to how it felt to be that young and to have your whole life in front of you without any worries. With both kids in college, it was their time to fly and as much as I would miss them, I had to let them find their own way, without our baggage holding them back.

I still find myself listening for any inflection in their voices. I try to read between the lines to make sure that the stress and pressures of being on their own does not become too overwhelming.

I feel guilty when I have to call on one of the kids to check on the other one. I try to tell myself that it is not their responsibility to be my eyes and ears out there, but sometimes the worry overwhelms me, and I have to call on them. As much as I want to, I can't ask them to betray any confidences between them. I do have faith that if one of them is in trouble, the other one will be there for them. When they were young, they fought like cats and dogs, but they have really grown up to be friends. They will tell more to each other than they would ever tell us. I am so grateful for that bond and maybe just a little bit envious. I miss the bond we shared as a family, and I feel like I let it slip through my fingers without even realizing it.

Time passes too quickly it seems. During many therapy sessions, I saw the errors I made in the way I handled their dad's depression with them. I spent so much time and effort trying to keep them from seeing how their dad was that they never realized how truly hard it had been. In shielding him, I was also shielding them from reality, this reality of working through problems and the reality that sometimes there is no easy answer. I have had many long conversations with them since, trying to explain why I held on so tightly and why I tried to protect them. I apologized for the mistakes I made along the way and asked for forgiveness. I wanted them to have a good life and good memories to carry with them. I had so many moments with just them, talking, laughing, and crying. I know that what we went through was not by choice, but I do treasure the bonds that we formed through it.

"He reached down from the heaven and
rescued me; he drew me out
of deep waters."
(2 Samuel 22:17)

*"He leads me beside peaceful streams. He renews my
strength." (Psalm 23:2–3)*

STILL WATERS

I feel like I have grown a lot in these past years. For every step forward, I have taken three steps back, but I am still trying. It has not been easy, and I won't tell you it will be.

I think that this illness is something that will always be with us in some form. We just have to choose how we are going to deal with it. Will it consume us or will we rise above it, renewed in strength? I don't have that answer yet.

"The LORD is my rock, my fortress, and my savior; my God is my rock, in whom I find protection. He is my shield, the power that saves me, and my place of safety" (Psalm 18:2).

When faced with an illness, at times you feel like you are the rock; at other times, you are the one clinging to that rock, and sometimes both of you are on the rock just clinging to each other. Sometimes all you can do is be there, hold their hand, and let your love, strength, and faith hold you both up. The need to comfort and to be comforted switching back and forth between you both. Praying for the strength to help the other one through whatever may come.

I still wait to see what's going to happen in our lives. Every morning when I wake up, I have to make a conscious decision that today I will not let his illness define me. I have had to search a long time to rediscover my joy of life, and I want to live the life that God has given me. I know that I am going to go through valleys, but there are going to be views from some mountaintops along the way.

I talk to both kids about what their dad and I have been going through. I hope they understand the tough decisions we have and may still have to make. I try to explain that I was not sure how much longer I could hold onto a marriage alone. Of course, no kid wants to hear that, but I had struggled so long by myself, and I need their help. I tell them that they need to help me out sometimes with their dad. I had shouldered the task of keeping things together for so long by myself that if they could step in when they see me overwhelmed, it would be a tremendous help. It wasn't easy opening up to them. I had held it in for so long, but I was afraid for us if I did not ask for their help. I don't know how much I will be willing to let them step in; after all, I am still the mom and that instinct to protect them is so strong. But sometimes you just have to let them see that you are human too and not too proud to ask for help. Yes, I worry that they may be prone to depression too, but I pray that by my being more open and honest with them that they will not be too proud to reach out to help another person or to seek help for themselves.

For now, we have made the joint decision to go forward each day, not forgetting the past, but learning from it, not living in the past, but looking to the future. I see a glimpse of the person my husband used to be come through occasionally—like a ray of sun through the clouds—and that gives me hope.

I am still holding my breath, fingers crossed, waiting, watching. I keep on because to stop is to give up on the person I love. Oftentimes, I am not sure if that is what I need or want to do. It would mean accepting the possibility that he will never be back. It is one of the hardest things I have ever had to do.

I highly recommend that you seek counseling both individually and as a couple. It has helped me to see the issues I have struggled with in the past and how they have affected how I deal, and have dealt, with this illness. While the joint sessions did help us see each other's side clearer, I realize now that the main reason we were there was *his* depression. It was primarily his session, and I was just there to discuss how it affected us both. Having a person to talk to on your own about *your* pain, *your* sadness, and *your* anger is a huge benefit. I wish I had known that then.

I hope that my husband finds the answers and reassurance he is searching for. I know now that I alone cannot give that to him. I hope that he finds himself again, not just for us as a couple, but for peace for him.

We have also found a wonderful church that is accepting of everyone despite of, and because of, their faults. It has helped us to realize that there are so many people out there going through their own personal trials, and so many people out there willing to listen or just hold your hand while you cry it out.

Realize that even though your loved one suffers with depression, that doesn't mean he or she can't live or make decisions. You can only control your feelings, not anyone else's. You can't fix anyone else either; that is not your job. His happiness should not control how you feel about yourself. Focus on the things you can do something about.

I don't know where this journey will lead me; I do know that it has brought me into a closer relationship with God, a relationship where I trust Him with my life. He has known the plans He has for my life since before I was born, and I must trust Him to work these things out for His good.

"For I know the plans I have for you," says the LORD. "They are plans for good and not for disaster, to give you a future and a hope" (Jeremiah 29:11).

I am learning to put my trust in God. That has been a hard lesson for me, as I have never trusted easily. He is the One who will never leave me nor forsake me. I can lean on Him. His love never changes.

You may hear people say a lot of things about depression. Don't take it personally. We know that until you've been through it or watched someone you love go through it, you just can't fully comprehend the hold it can have on your lives. People will say things about seeing a "shrink," popping "happy" pills, etc. Even well-meaning relatives can be hurtful and unthinking. Many people suffer in silence for that reason. I think it's time people quit hiding their struggles, quit trying to always put on a brave face, and start sharing how they feel. Maybe if more people are honest about what they are struggling with, other people would become less judgmental. What if everyone could talk about what they were going through without fear of reprisal? Wouldn't there be less prejudice and perhaps more solutions found?

Be grateful that you have learned to be more tolerant of people, to look beyond the surface, and know that behind every person you meet is a different side, a private side. Be glad that they have not had to go through this, but be grateful that you have learned that everyone must find his or her own way. Remember, there are two sides to every story, and the greatest thing is to offer support, not judgment. Perhaps by opening up and sharing our stories, we can start a change. If not in everyone at once, at least in us and the lives we touch.

"We prove ourselves by our purity, our understanding, our patience, our kindness, by the Holy Spirit within us, and by our sincere love" (2 Corinthians 6:6).

I realized that during this journey, I had lost pieces of me along the way, those qualities that made me, me. I have now realized that by constantly focusing on the next "winter" season, I could no longer recognize the beauty in every season of life. I have had to find me again. The new me, the me that could once again see the colors mixed with the grays. I could see promise and life in what lies ahead for me. I am still here for him, but I am trying not to let this time of our lives define the rest of mine. I finally have found the courage to be me—the good and the ugly, the nice and the mean, the silly and the sad, the selfish and the sympathetic. They are all me, and that's okay. I am not perfect, and I can finally give myself permission not to be. The world does not rest on my shoulders alone. We are all in this together, and if we stand shoulder to shoulder, we can carry the weight.

Can I tell you that you won't get tired? No. You will be exhausted, mentally and physically.

Can I tell you that you won't want to throw up your hands and give up? No. You will be tempted every day to run for the hills. But you won't; you stay. You know that if you give up on him, he will give up on himself. You are his lighthouse on the shore, giving him direction in his sea of darkness.

Can I tell you that you won't be angry that it's come back? No. I get angry every time depression shows up again.

I cannot tell you that your depression experience will be just like mine. All I know is that we keep on going, put it in God's hands, pray, and try to hold on until this current episode ends. Our individual details may be different, but others have been where you are now. I've been there. I understand the frustration, the grief, the anger, the sadness, and the desire to run. Yes, it is okay to feel that way. You are not being selfish. It does not mean that you do not love them. You would not still be here if you didn't. You wouldn't even have picked up this book. You would have left long ago—made a new life for yourself, away from the void. But you haven't. You are still hanging in there. You hope and you pray. You exist on the belief that things will get better. Hold on. Just hold on.

I don't know if you will get your old life back. Maybe not the one you had, but you will be stronger. You will make it. You are not alone. We are all in it together, living day by day, appreciative of a smile, a laugh, a hug.

I asked my husband if he remembered what normal was like. He thought for a minute and said no. Neither could I. Maybe that is the answer. Maybe this is our new normal. Normal is taking each day as it comes, good or bad, happy or sad. Normal is what you make it. Each day,

I have to make a conscious decision whether to follow him on his path or follow my own. I decide how I will feel today. And this story we call life continues. May God bless you and keep you.

INSPIRATIONS

——————————————————————————

"All Scripture is inspired by God and is useful to teach us what is true and to make us realize what is wrong in our lives. It corrects us when we are wrong and teaches us to do what is right" (2 Timothy 3:16).

I pray this book will give you some comfort and strength.

If you know someone dealing with a loved one's depression or chronic illness and you felt this book helped you in some way, please share this with them.

Please remember these few things:

- Don't hesitate to ask for help. Go alone if the other person cannot or will not go.

- Remember, you are not alone. Sometimes God has a way of opening our eyes to others around us. You will begin to recognize that sad look in other people now. You will recognize it in other people's voices. You will see the signs much quicker now, and try to be there if they need to talk. Maybe that is your part in all this.

- Be grateful every day for the life God has given you and this opportunity to learn, to help, to give love, to stand up for someone, and to be the strong person someone can lean on.

- When you feel the pressure building up, pick up a pen and write down how you feel. Keep a journal of your thoughts and feelings. Sometimes putting your thoughts down on paper helps you to let it go. They don't have to make sense or even be legible. Just the act of giving them an outlet is a release.

- Write down words and things that encourage you. Go back and read them when you need reassurance.

I have included just a few of the verses I have found that help me. I'm sure you will find many others along the way.

"And the Holy Spirit helps us in our weakness. For example, we don't know what God wants us to pray for. But the Holy Spirit prays for us with groaning that cannot be expressed in words" (Romans 8:26).

"But as for you, be strong and courageous, for your work will be rewarded" (2 Chronicles 15:7).

"The LORD is close to the brokenhearted; he rescues those whose spirits are crushed" (Psalm 34:18).

"I weep with sorrow; encourage me by your word" (Psalm 119:28).

"We can rejoice, too, when we run into problems and trials, for we know that they help us develop endurance. And endurance develops strength of character, and character strengthens our confident hope of salvation" (Romans 5:3–4).

"That is why we never give up. Though our bodies are dying, our spirits are being renewed every day. For our present troubles are small and won't last very long. Yet they produce for us a glory that vastly outweighs them and will last forever!" (2 Corinthians 4:16–17).

"Search for the LORD and for his strength; continually seek him" (1 Chronicles 16:11).

"He uncovers mysteries hidden in darkness; he brings light to the deepest gloom" (Job 12:22).

"The light shines in the darkness, and the darkness can never extinguish it" (John 1:5).

"Though they stumble, they will never fall, for the LORD holds them by the hand" (Psalm 37:24).

"Rejoice in our confident hope. Be patient in trouble, and keep on praying" (Romans 12:12).

"Trust in the LORD with all your heart; do not depend on your own understanding" (Proverbs 3:5).

"I have fought the good fight, I have finished the race, and I have remained faithful" (2 Timothy 4:7).

"And we know that God causes everything to work together for the good of those who love God and are called according to his purpose for them" (Romans 8:28).

"All praise to God, the Father of our LORD Jesus Christ. God is our merciful Father and the source of all comfort. He comforts us in all our troubles so that we can comfort others. When they are troubled, we will be able to give them the same comfort God has given us" (2 Corinthians 1:3–4).

And the one that I repeat most often:

"For I can do everything through Christ, who gives me strength" (Philippians 4:13).

ACKNOWLEDGMENTS

I want to thank my family and friends for supporting me on this journey. Without their prayers and encouragement, I don't think I could have made it this far. Thank you to the people at CRE8 2012 and Innovo Publishing for their belief in my manuscript. I would also like to thank my therapist for the encouragement to search for me again. Thank you to my pastor for always having the sermon that I needed to hear at just the right time. To my kids, thanks for forgiving my mistakes and loving me through it all. Thank you to my husband for continuing his fight and for his support in sharing this story. And to God, who, throughout this journey, has never left me nor forsaken me.

I am grateful that you had the strength to search out assistance and humbled that you chose to pick up my book and share in my story.

I pray that this book will be a stepping stone along your path—a path to finding yourself.

Additional Resources

I know when I first started dealing with my husband's illness, I was overwhelmed by the many Web sites I found when I searched for depression. I just gave up before looking at them closer.

Once I was able to search more in depth, I found so much helpful information, and I want to share it with you.

Each of the people I spoke with shared a great desire to help people who were dealing with mental illness from both the depressed individual and the caregiver.

Please check out these Web sites:

www.MentalHealthMinistries.net

The mission of Mental Health Ministries is to provide educational resources to help erase the stigma of mental illness in our faith communities and help congregations become caring congregations for persons living with a mental illness and their families. Their video clips and their email spotlights offer helpful and encouraging information.

www.dbsalliance.org

Depression and Bipolar Support Alliance offers inspiration, empowerment, information, and support.

DBSA envisions wellness for people who live with depression and bipolar disorder. Because DBSA was created for and is led by individuals living with mood disorders, their vision, mission, and programming are always informed by the personal, lived experience of peers. Their twenty-four-hour helpline is 1-800-273-TALK.

www.nami.org
National Alliance on Mental Illness focuses on support, education, research, and advocacy to help individuals and families affected by mental illness. NAMI is steadfast in its commitment to raising awareness and building a community of hope for all of those in need. They offer education, family-to-family, and peer-to-peer courses. Their helpline is 1 (800) 950 NAMI or (6264).